Walking Victoriously

Dr. Byron C. Hayes

authorHOUSE®

AuthorHouse™
1663 Liberty Drive
Bloomington, IN 47403
www.authorhouse.com
Phone: 1-800-839-8640

Unless otherwise indicated, all scripture quotations are
taken from King James Version of the Bible.

First published by AuthorHouse   8/17/2010

ISBN: 978-1-4520-5844-3 (sc)
ISBN: 978-1-4520-5846-7 (e)

Library of Congress Control Number: 2010911878

Printed in the United States of America
Bloomington, Indiana

This book is printed on acid-free paper.

Contents

Introduction

In the battles of life, "What next?", one might ask. However, in this book *"Walking Victoriously"*, we, as the Church (The Body of Christ) face daily warfare, tests and trials and as the Church we need to know and understand in this day of perplexity and war that we need to come from a relaxed state of mind. It is time the Church take the dark glasses of denial off, acting as if battles don't exist.

We, the Body of Christ, have a battle in the spirit realm *(Ephesians 6)*. We realize the battle is against the forces of darkness, principalities, powers, rulers and wickedness in high places. Paul says in the book of Ephesians, chapter six,

"Put on the whole armour of God,

that ye may be able to stand

against the wiles of the devil."

Throughout this book you will find the need for **walking victoriously** in your life. The devil knows his time is short *(Revelation 12:12)*. I trust this book to be a blessing to you as you prayerfully read the printed pages which the Holy Spirit has allowed me to complete.

Chapter 1
"Walking Victoriously"

"Finally, my brethren, be strong in the Lord, and in the power of his might. Put on the whole armour of God, that ye may be able to stand against the wiles of the devil. For we wrestle not against flesh and blood, but against the rulers of the darkness of this world, against spiritual wickedness in high places."

...Ephesians 6:10-12

I have heard often the statement used by the church in time past, "The devil made me do it:, which is a statement so far from the truth and a *"Big Lie"* from the devil. I found that the devil would love to make comedians out of God's people. *"Be sober, be vigilant; because your adversary, the devil, as a roaring lion, walketh about, seeking whom he may devour"* *(I Peter 5:8)*. This is why the study of *"Walking Victoriously"* is so important in this hour of the church realizing that this is the darkest hour of human history ever known to mankind.

The prince of this world *(Satan)* is not joking with the Body of Christ *(the church)*. And besides, Hell is no laughing matter. Church, this is the time to put our priorities and perspectives in order. Jesus said, *Hereafter, I will not talk much with you: For the prince of this world cometh, and hath nothing in me"* *(St. John 14:30)*.

We, as God's people have victory over Satan's kingdom. *"Behold, I give unto you power to tread* (walk) *on serpents and scorpions, and over all the power of the enemy: and nothing shall by any means hurt you"* *(St. Luke 10:19)*.

In our key verse of this first chapter on spiritual warfare, Paul tells us in the book *(letter)* of Ephesians, which is the New Testament Handbook on spiritual warfare, that we have the power over the devil and his kingdom. For it was Martin

Luther that wrote, *"A mighty fortress is our God, a bulwark never failing; our helper He, amid the flood of mortal ills prevailing."*

We, as the Body of Christ *(The Church)* need to understand that subjective feelings, emotional desires and fervent sincerity are not sufficient weaponry against Satan's war. In spiritual warfare, we must know true weaponry. The devil retreats or runs only from the Name *"Jesus"* and the word *"Jesus"*.

Jesus said, *"It is written, Man shall not live by bread alone, but by every word that proceedeth out of the mouth of God" Matthew 4:4).* In this hour, we the Church need to know that we are loosed from Satan's claws and bondage because and only because of the *"Blood"* of Jesus Christ.

The Word of God points out three enemies that we need to look at: *(1)* The World (2) The Flesh and (3) The Devil; and these three enemies seek to defeat our spiritual life if we let them. Jesus said, *"The thief* (Devil) *cometh not, but for to steal, and to kill, and to destroy: I am come that they might have life, and that they* (Body of Christ) *might have it more abundantly"* *(St. John 10:10).* That's why it's vital and necessary that we know who we are in Jesus Christ. And not only know who we are, but also know our rights and authority.

"Therefore, if any man be in Christ,
he is a new creature:
old things are passed away, all things are become new."
...(II Corinthians 5:17)

It's a fact that you and I must know and understand that when we become believers in Christ Jesus *(born again)* our relationship to everything in the (1) physical, (2) spiritual and (3) mental and emotional world undergo a radical change.

Yes, we become *"new"* creations and everything becomes new. We, as believers become citizens of Heaven. *"Wherefore, holy brethren, partakers of the heavenly calling, consider the Apostle and High Priest of our profession, Christ Jesus"* *(Hebrews 3:1).*

It's a fact the devil tries to hide this truth from the Church. *"In whom the god of this world* (Satan) *hath blinded the minds of them which believe not, lest the light of the glorious gospel of Christ, who is the image of God, should shine unto them"* *(II Corinthians 4:4).* This is not a negative statement but a fact "we" as believers are marked targets by the enemy, but *"When the enemy (Satan) shall come in like a flood the spirit (word) of the Lord shall lift up a standard against him"* *(Isaiah 59:19).*

We, the Body of Christ must know all we can about the available defense we have in the Word *(Logos)* of God. *"My people are destroyed for lack of knowledge" (Hosea 4:6)*. If earthly military make careful preparation, how much more should we, the Church?

The fact remains the believer who does not become familiar with spiritual warfare will indeed be a poor soldier of Jesus Christ. *"This charge I commit unto thee, son Timothy, according to the prophecies which went before on thee, that thou by them mightest war a good "warfare" (I Timothy 1:18)*.

Let us remember the world, the flesh and the devil must be challenged and defeated by the victory *"won"* for us through our Lord Jesus Christ.

> *"Ye are of God, little children, and have overcome them:*
> *Because greater is He (God) that is in you (Spirit man)*
> *than he (devil) that is in the world."*
> *...I John 4:4*

Using God's Word is the principle ingredient for **walking victoriously**, Why? Because God's Word is POWER!

Chapter 2
"Walking Victoriously in Spiritual Warfare"

"For they that are after the (flesh) do mind the things of the flesh; but they that are after the spirit the things of the spirit. For to be carnally minded is death, but to be spiritually minded is life and peace. Because the carnal mind is emnity against God; for it is not subject to the law of God, neither indeed can be. So they that are in the (flesh) cannot please God. But ye are not in the (flesh), but in the spirit, if so be that the spirit of God dwell in you. Now if any man have not the spirit of Christ, he is none of his."
... Romans 8:5-9

Much can be said about warfare with the (flesh) and (mind). Paul, a very educated, professional and spiritual man, made a very powerful statement for hurting men and women of our day in Romans, Chapter 7 verse 15. He says *"For that which I do I allow not: for what I would, that do I not; but what I hate, that do I."* How many times when we were not born again we made this statement? Or done this evil to ourselves not having knowledge that this was and is spiritual warfare. The devil was making us slaves to sin because we had no control in the Word of God! Or knowledge and understanding in the Word. How important the Word *(logos)* of God is to us in this dark age of sin, sickness, etc. Our *"sinful nature"* that we once had before becoming born again did not arise out of our original constitution, nor was it a result of our environment. Our sin nature resulted from our departure from God at one time in our lives. *"For when we were in the flesh, the motions of sins, which were by the law, did work in our members to bring forth fruit unto death."* (Romans 7:5).

Please don't forget, we inherited this time of bad hardship in our lives through *"Adam"* and *"Eve","* and the Lord God called unto Adam, and said unto him, where art thou? and he said,

I heard thy voice in the garden, and I was afraid, because I was naked; and I hid myself. And God said, who told thee that thou was naked? Hast thou eaten of the tree, whereof I commanded thee that thou shouldest not eat? And the man (Adam) said, the woman (Eve) whom thou gavest to be with me, she (Eve) gave me of the tree, and I did eat. And the Lord God said unto the woman (Eve), what is this that thou hast done? And the woman said, the serpent (devil) beguiled me, and I (Eve) did eat." (Genesis 3:9-13).

Because of this fall we were described and identified as the *"old man"*, but thank God we are described and identified now as the *"new man"* in Christ Jesus because of the *"blood"* of Christ. One of the most common new testament words used to identify man's fallen nature is the word flesh. The great struggle and warfare that the believer has with the fallen nature is called the flesh. Along with that the Bible also speaks about the *"fleshy"* mind which is another danger zone, better known as the *"carnal"* mind; and this danger zone is enmity against God; this type of mind is not *"subject" to the law* (word) *of God,* neither indeed can be. So then they that are

9

in flesh cannot and will not please God. Body of Christ listen to me, I found in studying about the flesh that it is a built-in-law of *"failure"* making it impossible for man to please or serve God. The flesh can never be reformed or improved, unless the spirit man has been born again, and then the born again believer must present him or herself to the Lord as a living (total) sacrifice, holy, acceptable unto God, which is our reasonable service (Romans 12:1-2).

Man's flesh (old-man), his fallen nature has definite ways in which it tempts and always war against the spiritual man. *"But I see another law in my members, warring against the law of my mind, and bringing me into captivity to the law of sin which is in my members." (Romans 7:23).* We, the church need to understand that the flesh is a *"deadly"* enemy which is capable of completely defeating a believer and keeping him from pleasing God with a holy life. If the believer lets it happen, the *"Zoe"* life which means the God kind of life, will prevent many problems that spring from the *(flesh)*, the old man such as **adultery**, *fornication, uncleanness, lasciviousness, murders, drunkenness, revellings and such like (Galatians 5:19-21).* This is why in spiritual warfare we thank God for the *(1) Word (2) Holy Spirit (3) Blood of Jesus (4) Angels (5) and Body of Christ.* Thank God we as the church have the absolute *"victory"* over such temptations, that war against believers. By all means let us not forget this world is no longer the natural habitat for men and women who have been born again. The Body of Christ is a citizen of Heaven. Praise God!

"But having seen them afar off, and were persuaded of them, and embraced them, and confessed that they were strangers and pilgrims on the earth. For they that say such things declare plainly that they seek a country, and truly, if they had been mindful of that country from whence they came out, they might have had opportunity to have returned. But now they desire a (better) country, that is, a (Heavenly); wherefore God is not ashamed to be called their God; for he hath prepared for them a City (Hebrews 11:13-16)" It is a fact this world is not our home, Glory to God!

Now, there are three Greek words which translate the word (world): *(1) oikoumene (2) aion (3) kosmos.* The one I teach often is the translation *"kosmos"* and this of course is where our enemy lives and has rules. *"Where in time past ye walked according to the course of this world, according to the prince of the power of the air, the spirit that now worketh in the children of disobedience."* (Ephesians 2:2). Satan and man's flesh have a vital partnership in formulating the world system in its activities and philosophies. *"The world system begins to surround man with that which intensifies the inner problem he already has as a fallen creature."* I found Satan's main tool for defeat in the believer's life is the world and with this tool he tries to cause defeat with the church. I found in spiritual warfare study that the devil has a very highly organized kingdom that seeks to rule over the world system *if* we allow him space or room. *"And the Lord said unto Satan, whence comest thou? Then Satan answered the Lord and said "From going to and fro in the earth, and from walking up and down in it." (Job 1:7)* The world system is marked by many of Satan's most *vicious* attacks against God and against the Body of Christ. Remembering Satan's prime target is to get us to think contrary to God's will, then we've fallen into its trap and then we become worldly. The world always has specific ways to try to tempt us as God's people called *"ADVERTISING,"* and this should not fool us. Also, the world uses gain, greed, power, position, honor and advantage to try to trick us, so we in the body of Christ must know spiritual warfare in the *"kosmos".* As believers, we must know that in Jesus we can handle the world's tricks, and temptations and walk before them in total victory, *Praise God!*

The word of God is our only inspired book on spiritual warfare. *"For the word of God is quick, and powerful, and sharper than any two-edged sword, piercing even to the dividing asunder of soul and spirit and of the joints and marrow, and is a discerner of the thoughts and intents of the heart" (Hebrews 4:12).* I find other books are useful only as they are in harmony with the Word of God. Jesus in the 4th chapter of Matthew, when waging battle with the devil used nothing but the Word of God. That is why spiritual warfare should be developing upon growing use of the Bible.

The word must be put in us, and by in us, I mean our spirit man. *"Thy word have I hid in mine heart, that I might not sin against thee." (Psalm 119:11) "This is why in waging spiritual warfare scripture memorization and meditation are so important. This book of the law shall not depart out of thy mouth; but thou shall meditate there in day and night, that thou mayest observe to do according to all that is written there in; for then thou shalt make thy way prosperous, and then thou shalt have good success." (Joshua 1:8)*

"But his delight is in the law of the Lord; and in his law doth he meditate day and night." (Psalm 1:2).

I find that no one will become strong in spiritual warfare who neglects using the Word of God in an active program of memorization and meditation. *"I have esteemed the words of his mouth more than my necessary food." (Job 23:12).*

In the body of Christ, the church, we know that the Word of God is God's medicine for all manner of spiritual ills. It works like the doctor's medicine. The more you take in, the better it works. This is why a Christian must stay *"victorious"*. He is constantly taking in the Word and he knows it is working within him to do all the good things he or she needs. The Word is medicine; *"My son, attend to my words incline thine ear unto my sayings, let them not depart from thine eyes; keep them in the midst of thine heart for they are life (medicine) unto those that find them, and health (medicine to all their flesh)." (Proverbs 4:20-22).* Memorization and meditation upon the Word of God is perhaps the greatest step a believer can take in helping himself or herself overcome the world and also the flesh and also the devil. As a help to spiritual warfare, the church should know the original state in which Satan was created. Full of wisdom and beauty, he was given a place on God's holy mountain. He was created a holy and righteous being. Pride in his heart was the beginning of his fall, and then there was Satan's rebellion and fall in which we shall never forget. Lucifer fought to exhalt himself to the position of JEHOVAH. Also, in the devil's vanity, he declared *"I will be like God."* Then there came the names of the devil; his many names which describe his activity, showing him to be a *"devious enemy"*. The name Satan means *"adversary"*. He is the accuser of the brethren. The name Lucifer means *"light bearer"*, and this is where we have to be very careful. Why? Because the devil comes as an angel of light to deceive the people of God, the very elect, if we are not careful. So we see there are many names the devil has: the dragon, the slanderer, the murderer, the liar, the deceiver, prince of this world, prince of power of the air, the destroyer, the tempter, the evil one, etc., but even when we complete his names, Jesus is still and always will be King of Kings and Lord of Lords. Jesus is Alpha and Omega, the Beginning and Ending, which is, and which was, and which is to come, the Almighty. He is the Great I Am. He is alive for ever more and he has the keys of hell and death *(Revelation 1:8, 1:11, 1:18)*. In the body of Christ how greatly important it is to see that Satan backs off from nothing but the absolute truth and fact of God's word. It is not enough to know sound doctrine. We must use it and apply it in our daily walk with God. Every truth of God's Word is given to us not just to know, but to use for God's glory and our victory. Continual aggressiveness is the walk of warfare in the kingdom walk of God. Remember, our victory rests only in the *"it is written"*. The Holy Spirit and the whole armour is absolutely essential to victorious spiritual warfare over Satan.

Walking Victoriously in prayer and faith in spiritual warfare, aggressive prayer always wins. I find if we use God's mighty weapons, not those made by man, to knock down the devil's strong holds, these weapons can break down every proud argument against God and every wall that can be built to keep men from finding Him. You see, the word "aggressive" means offensive, distressing, pushy and afflicting. So, in walking victorious, God wants **his** people pushy in the word because the word has power, it is a fact that in this last hour of human history, Christian parents have broken hearts because of rebellious, sin-bound children who seem to be in bondage to Satan. Why? because of no aggressive prayer or faith of their own. So if we want joyful results in our Christian life, let's look into warfare praying with aggressive faith and **Walking Victoriously**. I found in my Christian walk, that Satan will go to almost any length to divert the body of Christ from prayer, faith, and victory. When we in the church understand that the devil is just symptoms, we can walk in victory. Body of Christ, God is calling the church to "bull-dog" faith, and "bull-dog" power. It is important to be bold and direct in applying the weapons of our warfare to our own marriage and the home. As pastoring a church for 23 ½ years, I see now that if Satan's kingdom can keep a husband and wife from loving each other according to God's will and way, he will not only ruin them, but also will destroy their children's lives as well. So this is why the devil does not want *"aggressive"* prayer in the home, the church, or on the job. Why? because it is a mighty, mighty part of the believers effectiveness in spiritual warfare and **Walking Victoriously**. Be clothed in the whole armour of God, stop depending upon your own strength! God does not intend for you to face your financial burdens, physical sicknesses, or problems in your family in your own limited understanding or your own strength. He has planned a purpose for you to face every problem, every circumstance, every attack of the enemy in his **unlimited**, unsurpassed power! We must put on God's complete armour. Everything Jesus did, he did in the strength and power of almighty God. He did not depend upon his own strength. When he healed the sick, cast out demons, opened blind eyes and raised the dead, he drew upon the almighty power of God. Jesus said, *"The Father that dwelleth in me, he doeth the works." (John 14:10).* Jesus knew that the great I Am was with him, dwelling in him, working through him. He said, *"I and my father are one." (John 10:30)... "the Father is in me, and I in him" (John 10:38).* When Jesus faced Satan and all the forces of hell, he drew upon the power of almighty God on the cross. He was not depending upon his own strength to resurrect him from the dead. He faced death knowing a powerful source, the spirit of the living God within him, would raise him from the dead. That same mighty power that was working within Jesus that broke the chains of death and raised him from the dead, is at work - right now - within you! Paul prayed that the Ephesians would know and understand the *immeasurable,* unlimited and unsurpassed greatness of his power in us and for us! Glory to God!

Chapter 3
"Walking Victoriously in Faith, Not Fear"

"Wherefore take unto you the whole armor of God, that ye may be able to withstand in the evil day, and having done all to stand, stand therefore, having your loins girt about with truth, and having on the breast plate of righteousness; and your feet shod with the preparation of the gospel of peace; above all, taking the shield of faith, wherewith ye shall be able to quench all the fiery darts of the wicked. And take the helmet of salvation, and the sword of the spirit, which is the word of God; praying always with all prayer and supplication in the spirit, and watching there unto with all perseverance and supplication for all saints."
...(Ephesians 6:13-18)

Born again believers need to consider our warfare against Satan. One extreme must carefully be avoided, and that is to ignore that the devil exist. It is erroneous to think such a thing. The devil does exist along with his kingdom. Don't be fooled by his strategy to make us more conscious and aware of himself and his kingdom than we are of the heavenly Father and His kingdom. So let us as the church be careful of the fact that God's kingdom is bigger and better on every hand for the believers. *"And blessed be his glorious name forever; and let the whole earth be filled with his glory. Amen and amen."* *(Psalm 72:19).*

It is very common as a problem in the body of Christ for those under the attack of Satan to become preoccupied with thoughts about how Satan is tempting, afflicting, or oppressing them rather than *"meditating on the victory Christ has won"*. It is the will of God for (**all**) believers to be victorious. We are to remain strong and powerful until Jesus returns for the Church. *(Revelation 3:11-3:21).*

Now there are other important teachings along the lines of spiritual warfare such as the spirit of *"fear"*. The attack of *"fear"* comes in the strategy of *"phobias"*. If the devil can't get you one way, he will come another way. He'll use such *"phobias"* as:

ailurophobia, *"fear of cats"* • algophobia, *"fear of pain"*

androphobia, *"fear of men"* • anemphobia, *"fear of winds or drafts"*

aphephobia, *"aversion to being touched by people"*

arachnophobia, *"fear of spiders"*

astrephobia, *"fear of thunderstorms"*

astrophobia, *"fear of the sky, its mystery"*

autophobia, *"fear of being alone"* • basiphobia, *"fear of walking"*

bathophobia, *"fear of falling from high places"*

batophobia, *"fear of high objects (towers, mountains)"*

carphobia, *"fear of insects"*

coprophobia, *"repugnance to filth and dirt"*

cynophobia, *"fear of dogs"* • demophobia, *"fear of crowds"*

doraphobia, *"fear of touching animal hair or fur"*

ergasiophobia, *"dislike of work, taking responsibilities"*

gamophobia, *"fear of marriage"*

gehrophobia, *"fear of crossing bridge over water"*

gynephobia, *"fear of women"* • necrophobia, *"fear of dead bodies"*

nudophobia, *"fear of being seen unclothed"*

ophidiophobia, *"fear of harmless snakes"*

pantophobia, *"fear of future"* • pharmacophobia, *"fear of medicine"*

photophobia, *"fear of light"* • psychrophobia, *"fear of cold"*

pyrophobia, *"fear of fire"* • rhabdophobia, *"fear of being beaten"*

scopophobia, *"fear of being watched"*

scotophobia, *"fear of darkness"* • sitophobia, *"fear of eating"*

toxicophobia, *"fear of being poisoned"*

zoophobia, *"fear of animals in general"*.

No believer should be fearful. No where in God's word are believers taught to fear. They are taught the exact opposite. God gives you a spirit of power, a spirit of love and spirit of a sound mind. The spirit of fear is just like "cancer", it eats, and eats, and eats until if you are not careful, you are robbed of God's best.

The Spirit of fear has no respect of person, it comes like a lion *(I Peter 5:8)*. Fear attacks a small baby to a ninety nine year old man. Fear has no respect of person. It's a fact this spirit does not come from God. *"Fearfulness"* is not God. *There is no fear in love; but perfect love casteth out fear; because fear hath torment. He that feareth is not made perfect in love." (I John*

4:18). The Holy Spirit is not one who makes us fearful, rather he gives us spiritual power, a heart of love and a mind that is sound and understanding. *"For God hath not given us the spirit of fear, but of power, and of love, and of a sound mind."* *(II Timothy 1:7).* *"Yea, though I walk through the valley of the shadow of death, I will fear no evil; for thou art with me, thy rod and thy staff, they comfort me."* *(Psalm 23:4).* We should always understand that fear comes from another spirit. Who? Satan and his demons, of course; for they are the authors of fear. Of course fear is the opposite of faith. Fear will cause death if we let it take advantage of us. *"Fear numbs and dulls our alertness and has the capacity to make us freeze in terror if we let it".* It is said that a roar of a lion can actually paralyze his prey that he stalks, yes the devil can create fear in the body of Christ if the door of doubt is left open. As people of God, we should never avoid the subject of spiritual warfare. That's what **WALKING VICTORIOUSLY** is all about. As the Church of Jesus Christ stay blood washed, blood bought, blood kept, we cannot be moved. Glory to God! Now we have victories over all enemies *(Isaiah 54:17 - 59:19).* Fear is one of the strong ways in which Satan controls mankind. The sword of the spirit spoken, which is the word of God, will destroy this **strong man,** the devil called fear. Let's walk victoriously standing against the spirit of fear in the word of God, on your mark, get set, GO!

Deuteronomy 31:8 - *"And the Lord, he it is that doth go before thee; he will be with thee, he will not fail thee, neither forsake thee; fear not, neither be dismayed.*

Psalm 23:4 - *"Yea, though I walk through the valley of the shadow of death, I will fear no evil, for thou art with me, thy rod and thy staff they comfort me."*

Psalm 27:1 - *"The Lord is my light and my salvation; whom shall I fear? The Lord is the strength of my life; of whom shall I be afraid?"*

Psalm 34:4 - *"I sought the Lord, and he heard me, and delivered me from all my fears."*

Pslam 91:5 - *"Thou shalt not be afraid for the terror by night; nor for the arrow that flieth by day."*

Proverbs 18:10 - *"The name of the Lord is a strong tower; the righteous runneth into it, and is safe."*

Isaiah 41:10 - *"Fear thou not; for I am with thee; be not dismayed; for I am thy God; I will strengthen thee; yea, I will help thee; yea, I will uphold thee with the right hand of my righteousness."*

Matthew 28:20 - *"...Lo, I am with you always, even unto the end of the world."*

Luke 12:7 - *"But even the very hairs of your head are all numbered, fear not therefore; ye are of more value than many sparrows."*

Romans 8:15 - *"For ye have not received the spirit of bondage again to fear;..."*

II Thessalonians 3:3 - *"But the Lord is faithful, who shall stablish you, and keep you from evil."*

II Timothy 1:7 - *"For God hath not given us the spirit of fear; but of power, and love, and of a sound mind."*

I John 4:18 - *"There is no fear in love; but perfect love casteth out fear..."*

Revelation 21:7-8 - *"He that overcometh shall inherit all things; and I will be his God, and he shall by my son. But the fearful and unbelieving, and abominable, ...shall have their part in the lake which burneth with fire and brimstone; which is the second death."*

Chapter 4
"The Devil, Demons and Demonic Powers"

The "I Will" fall of Lucifer...
"For thou hast said in thine heart, (I) will ascend into
heaven, (I) will exalt my throne above the stars of God:
(I) will sit also upon the mount of the congregation, in the
sides of the north." ...(Isaiah 14:13-14). Lucifer's fall from
heaven... "And the seventy returned again with joy, saying,
Lord, even the devils are subject unto us through thy
name. And he said unto them, I beheld Satan as lightning
fall from heaven. Behold, I give unto you power to tread
on serpents and scorpions, and over all the power of the
enemy: and nothing shall by any means hurt you. ...(Luke
10:17-19). *Satan's names reveal his nature and character...*

(A) Adversary - I Peter 5:8

(B) Thief - St. John 10:10

(C) Murderer and Liar - St. John 8:44

(D) Accuser of the Brethren - Revelation 12:10

(E) Deceiver - Revelation 12:9

(F) Angel of Light - II Corinthians 11:14

(G) The Prince of This World - John 12:31, 14:30, 16:8, 11

(H) Prince of the Power of the Air - Ephesians 2:2

(I) The God of This World System - II Corinthians 4:4

"If people understand that Satan is the god of this world, it would clear up a lot of confusion they have about why evil exists on this earth."

Satan took possession of man's lost dominion *(Genesis 3:6-7)* so this statement is true *(Luke 4:5-6)*. Is there three "heavens"? *(II Corinthians 12:2-4)*. The first of three heavens right above us is what we call the *"atmospheric heavens"*, or the *"heavenlies"*. Beyond that out in space, is the region where the stars, sun, moon and planets are - stellar heavens or space - which can be referred to as the second heaven, out beyond that, further than science knows about or has been able to explore, is the third heaven - the heaven of heavens - where God's throne is located. Paradise is located in this third heaven **(Luke**

23:43, II Corinthians 12:4, Revelation 2:7). We know Jesus is in heaven at the right hand of God **(Mark 16:19, Hebrews 1:3, 4:14)**. Look at the *contrast* between the kingdom of darkness and God's kingdom of light...

> *(A) John 8:12*
>
> *(B) John 12:35-36, 46*
>
> *(C) Ephesians 5:14*
>
> *(D) Romans 13:12*
>
> *(E) II Corinthians 6:14*
>
> *(F) I John 1:5-7*

Glory to God! Demon powers have no authority to rule over believers who walk in the light of God's word and give Satan no access. Believers can walk in the light so they won't fall prey to Satan. In fact, as believers gain knowledge of God's word, light and liberty come. The knowledge of God's word brings light. *(Psalm 119:130)*, and it is the knowledge of God's word which sets us free in every area.

Spirit, Soul and Body Evil spirits are fallen beings or disembodied spirits. As disembodied spirits, they seek to inhabit man in order to have a greater range of expression. As fallen beings, evils spirits seek to oppress, obsess, and if possible, to possess mankind. *Man Is A Spirit* He is a spirit being. He has a soul, mind, will, emotions and he lives in a body. **(I Thessalonians 5:23, Hebrews 4:12)**. With my spirit, I contact the spiritual realm. With my soul, I contact the intellectual and emotional realm. With my body, I contact the physical realm. The soul of man:

> *James 1:21*
>
> *I Peter 1:22*
>
> *Psalm 23:3*
>
> *Philippians 4:6-8*
>
> *Philippians 2:5*
>
> *Isaiah 26:3*

Inner Healing

The term "inner healing" is really a misnomer, but you say wait a minute, Dr. Hayes. Yes, but if it is used to refer to healing in your spirit, because your spirit doesn't need healing ~ it has been recreated. If you needed healing or deliverance from hurts on the inside, it wouldn't be in your born-again spirit because it has been made brand new. No, it is your soul that needs the help! How are your going to get all of those hurts in your soul from the past healed? By thinking in line with Word!

Keeping your body subject to your spirit is one of the primary ways you protect yourself against the enemy, and

actually, it is one of your greatest defenses against Satan. The renewed *mind transforms you!*

(A) Romans 12:1-2

(B) Ephesians 4:23

(C) Joshua 1:8 *Much of what is called* demonic *activity is not caused by demons. Now don't get fearful, Dr. Hayes is not taking up for the devil. But it is actually the fruit of a believer's* redeemed, unrenewed *mind giving access to the devil because the mind is the doorway, through which the devil gains access to people.*

Nugget 1

Wrong thinking opens the door to the devil.

Nugget 2

Man's body referred to as a "house" (II Corinthians 5:1-4)

You must present your body as a living sacrifice to God (Romans 12:1)

You must crucify or mortify the deeds of the body

(Col.3:5)

3) You must keep your body under subjection to your spirit man - the inward man - the real man on the inside (I Corinthians 9:27)

Nugget 3

There is an inward man and an outward man!

II Corinthians 4:16

I Peter 3:3-4

I Corinthians 9:27

Nugget 4

Is it the devil or the flesh?

Put off (Ephesians 4:22-24)

Put on (Colossians 3:12-14)

Be ye not (Ephesians 4:26)

Nugget 5

The flesh has its own lusts and it is not the devil.

Romans 1:24-28

Ephesians 4:22

I Peter 2:11

James 1:13-15

Ephesians 2:3

Nugget 6

Crucify the (flesh) NOT self

Colossians 3:5

Romans 8:5-8, 12-14

Reference word: *Mortify - kill, become dead, cause to be dead, put to death, or subdue. (Galatians 5:24)*

Nugget 7

Jesus' remedy for "flesh" problems

Matthew 5:29-30

You can't cast the flesh out; you have to crucify or mortify the deed of the flesh.

Put the responsibility where it belongs. You may say what do you mean, Dr. Hayes? Well, you might say:

"God take the snuff!"

"God take the wine!"

"God take the dope!"

"God take the smokes!"

But, you must remember *he* doesn't dip, drink, shoot or smoke. But your flesh does so <u>you</u> "crucify" your flesh.

(Ephesians 2:1-3)

A *"spirit"* of gluttony demon or you?

(Proverb 23:2)A *"spirit"* of uncleanness demon or you?

(Colossians 3:5)A *"spirit"* of the world demon or you?

(James 4:4; Colossians 3:8)Can Christians *"yield"* to the devil?

(Romans 6:16; Matthew 16:2-23)

Do demons have *"personalities"*? Yes, they...

Talk (Matthew 12:44)

Think (Matthew 12:44)

Communicate (Matthew 12:45)

Suggestion: Satan's Tool

Many believers wonder how Satan is able to gain ground in their lives. The first place Satan starts to work is their mind, and one of Satan's greatest and most powerful weapons is the weapon of suggestion.

(Genesis 3:1-7) If the devil can get a place in your thought life, he can get a place in you.

Are Spirits Real?

Spirits of infirmity (Luke 13:11)

Dumb and deaf spirit (Mark 9:25)

Unclean spirit (Matthew 12:43; Mark 1:23; Luke 9:42)

Blind spirit (Matthew 12:22)

Familiar spirits (Leviticus 20:27; Isaiah 8:19, II Kings 23:24)

An angel of light (II Corinthians 11:14)

A lion (I Peter 5:8)

A dragon (Revelation 12:7-9)

A lying spirit (I Kings 22:22-23, II Chronicles 18:21-22)

Seducing spirit (I Timothy 4:1)

Binding spirit (Matthew 18:18)

Foul spirit (Mark 9:25, Revelation 18:2)

Jealous spirit (Numbers 5:14, 30)

Witchcraft spirit (Deuteronomy 29:26-27, Exodus 20:3, Exodus 22:18)

"The Devil, Demons and Demonic Powers" The devil is a spirit, but thank God for the victory over the devil (in Jesus' name)! *Matthew - 4:24; 8:16; 8:28-33; 9:32-34; 10:1 & 8; 12:22-30; 12:43-45; 13:39; 15:22; 17:14-19; 25:41*

John - 10:10; 10:20-21; 13:2; 13:27

Acts - 5:3; 5:16; 8:7; 8:9-11; 10:38; 13:8-11; 16:16-18; 19:12-18; 26:18

Romans - 16:20

I Corinthians - 5:1-5; 7:5; 10:20-21

II Corinthians - 2:11; 4:4; 6:14-17; 11:13-15; 12:7

Galatians 1:4

Ephesians - 4:25-27; 6:11-16

Colossians - 1:13-17; 2:15

I Thessalonians 2:18

II Thessalonians - 2:8-12

I Timothy - 1:20; 3:6-7; 4:1-5; 5:15

II Timothy - 2:24-26; 4:17-18

Hebrews 2:14-15

James 2:19; 4:7

I Peter - 5:8-9

II Peter - 2:9

I John - 3:8-10; 4:3-4

II John 1:7

Jude - 6-11

Revelation - 2:9-10; 2:13; 2:24; 3:9

CHAPTER 5
"Walking Victoriously in Success"

This book of the law shall not depart out of thy mouth; but thou shalt meditate therein day and night, that thou mayest observe to do according to all that is written therein; for then thou shalt make thy way prosperous, and then thou shalt have good success. Joshua 1:8

Let me introduce my 21 day victory and success plan, to help program you for daily successful living. It's time to come out of life's stupor, struggles and defeats. It's time to overcome stresses from panic-stricken issues, and overcome darts of depression, discouragement, dismay, distraction and despondency. It's time for more (God) dedication flourishing and developing in God's favor, without alarm and agitation. But being anxious in the things of God. Let's start with day one. Day One…(1) Begin overcoming the road blocks of fear… (2) Know that you will become what you see, feel, or say…(3) Break all chains that hold you down in life… Day Two…(1) You can't help people who refuse to change…(2) You will become your words…(3) Can you see the outcome, in the eye's of Faith? Day Three (1) Exercise your mouth with the positive (2) Prepare to always win!! (3) Diminish all doubts

Day Four

(1) Free Yourself from debt

(2) Ask God for what you want

(3) Cease comparing yourself to others

Day Five

(1) Clear all the clutter from your life

(2) Maximize your faith

(3) Restructure your thoughts

Day Six

(1) Increase your financial intelligence

(2) Eliminate emotional breakdowns

(3) Put an end to "Enabling"

Day Seven

(1) Focus like a winner & release stress

(2) Boost your faith energy

(3) Lower your blood pressure and overcome
   insomnia

Day Eight

(1) Program yourself for financial success

(2) Break undesirable habits of "Thought and Action"

(3) Develop more self-discipline and end all procrastination

Day Nine

(1) Don't let disaster keep you down

(2) Overcome your "BUTTON" pushers

(3) Keep the "still-standing" attitude

Day Ten

(1) Know that you can be an overcomer

(2) Begin refreshing your attitude

(3) Overcome the pains of your past

Day Eleven

(1) Remember excellence is key, to everyday living

(2) Overcome all personal encounters

(3) Say to yourself, I can not and will not "argue"

Day Twelve

(1) Stop being a "wounded-warrior" get up and
    fight

(2) Begin breaking the "worry" habit

(3) Let past issues go and begin to live

Day Thirteen

(1) Let it go and rest in the Lord

(2) Shake it off, God's (in) control

(3) You can make it!!!

Day Fourteen

(1) Know that you have "WORD" creating power
    inside you

(2) Improve your "inside" image, just be you!!!

(3) It's time to put off procrastinating,
    procrastination is a thief of your time

Day Fifteen

(1) Profit from your past, and learn from it!

(2) Face the facts with yourself

(3) Wrong words can become your battlefield

Day Sixteen

(1) You cannot help everybody so stop!!! And Live

(2) Stop enabling others and yourself

(3) Escape your valley of "HUMILIATIONS" Get
    over-it!

Day Seventeen

(1) Avoid "Toxic" attitudes from people

(2) Zero in on your stressor's

(3) Begin to secure your foundation

Day Eighteen

(1) Begin to nourish your body and get good sleep!

(2) Enjoy the "Present" moment and be flexible

(3) Start resolving conflicts, learn to delegate

Day Nineteen

(1) Release the past, and move to the future

(2) Take "A" time out when needed

(3) Face your mistakes and shortcoming, be honest
    with you!

Day Twenty

(1) Limit all contact with stress- producing people

(2) Learn to create a peaceful atmosphere

(3) Release all your tension and start living

Day Twenty-One

(1) You need to laugh! It's Healing

(2) Stop stress speaklng

(3) Deal with your disappointments, in the eye's of

Faith

www.ingramcontent.com/pod-product-compliance
Lightning Source LLC
Chambersburg PA
CBHW050345290526
45785CB00006B/2647